Author:

John Malam studied ancient history and archaeology at the University of Birmingham, after which he worked as an archaeologist at the Ironbridge Gorge Museum, Shropshire. He is now an author, specialising in information books for children. He lives in Cheshire with his wife, a book designer, and their two children.

Artist:

Dave Antram was born in Brighton, England, in 1958. He studied at Eastbourne College of Art and then worked in advertising for 15 years before becoming a full-time artist. He has illustrated many children's non-fiction books.

Series creator:

David Salariya was born in Dundee, Scotland. He has illustrated a wide range of books and has created and designed many new series for publishers both in the U.K. and overseas. In 1989 he established The Salariya Book Company. He lives in Brighton with his wife, the illustrator Shirley Willis, and their son.

Editor:

Karen Barker Smith

Created, designed and produced by
The Salariya Book Company Ltd
25 Marlborough Place,
Brighton BN1 1UB

Published in Great Britain in 2000 by Hodder Wayland, an imprint of Hodder Children's Books

A catalogue record for this book is available from the British Library.

ISBN 0 7500 3067 4

Printed and bound in Italy

Hodder Children's Books
A division of Hodder Headline Limited
338 Euston Road, London NW1 3BH

You Wouldn't Want To Be A Roman Gladiator!

Gory things you'd rather not know

Written by
John Malam

Illustrated by
David Antram

Created and designed by
David Salariya

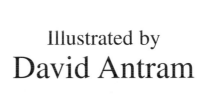

HODDER
Wayland

an imprint of Hodder Children's Books

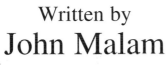

Contents

Introduction

It is the 1st century AD and you live in a village in the Roman province of Gallia, which covers a large area of northern Europe. You don't like the Romans much, and they don't like you or your people. The fact is the Romans invaded your territory more than 100 years ago, as they have done in many places, to build up the huge Roman Empire. They plan on ruling over you for a long time to come and say your people are uncivilised. They call you 'barbarians', meaning that you are different to them. The Romans believe they are much better than you.

From time to time some of your people pick a fight with the Romans. But you're no match against the Roman army. If you're not killed in battle, then don't expect to be shown any mercy, you'll be taken prisoner and marched off to the city of Rome. If you survive the long journey you face an uncertain future. Will you be sold as a slave to a rich Roman citizen or will you be sent to work in the mines? Will you end up doing hard labour in the quarries or will you sail around the Roman Empire as a galley slave?

Your fate is out of your control, but you can be sure of one thing – you wouldn't want to be a Roman gladiator!

Gotcha! Romans get their man

Goodbye to your former life:

THE ROMAN ARMY has invaded Gallia. The Romans want to make it part of their growing empire, but first they must defeat troublemakers. The Gauls, the people of Gallia, live in many different tribes. Some tribes are happy for the Romans to be their rulers but others fight them.

WEAPONS. The Romans will destroy your weapons – your bronze shield, iron sword and dagger, and slingshot.

JEWELLERY. The Romans will take your gold neckring, or torque, and bronze bracelets.

HORSE AND CHARIOT. The Romans will take your horses and smash your chariot.

HOME AND FAMILY. You may never see them again.

I hate Romans!

6

The Roman soldiers wear armour and follow a carefully worked-out battle plan. The Gauls are not so well organised. The fighting is soon over and unfortunately for you your tribe lose the battle. Captured Gauls have their weapons taken away and the fittest become prisoners of war. You are one of the prisoners and you are about to begin a new life.

Handy hint

Before the battle, offer a gift to your gods by throwing a weapon into a bog. This is the entrance to their underground world.

What next?

Prisoners are chained at the neck and led away to begin a new life as slaves.

I hate Gauls!

Prisoners are marched hundreds of miles from Gallia to Rome, the heart of the Roman Empire.

GALLIA

ROME

7

Sold! A slave market in Rome

It's a hard life for a slave:

DOWN THE MINES. Some slaves are sent to work in mines. They may never see daylight again.

QUARRYING. Slaves also work in the heat and dust of quarries, breaking rock for buildings and sculptures.

GALLEY SLAVES. Some men will become galley slaves, rowing the Roman navy's fighting ships and being whipped if they stop.

FARMING. Slaves on farms work in all weathers to grow food for the Romans.

AFTER CAPTURE by the army you are passed on to a slave-dealer, who buys and sells slaves. The dealer takes you to a slave market where you stand on a platform for everyone to see. Slaves with diseases are made to hold a sign so that people know there is something wrong with them. Chalk dust is sprinkled on your feet as a sign that you are a slave. The slave-dealer asks people to call out prices and he will sell you to the person who pays the most.

Before   After

A NEW MAN. Your new owner plans to turn you from a *Gallia comata*, Latin meaning a 'hairy Gaul', into a civilised Roman gladiator.

Oh no! Gladiators go to school

Are you ready for this?

NEW ARRIVAL. Your owner will hand you over to a trainer – a tough man who will teach you how to be a gladiator.

YOU ARE NOW the property of a wealthy Roman citizen. He's decided you will be sent to a *ludus gladiatorius* – a school where slaves, criminals and other wretches are trained to fight as gladiators. Once inside, the gates will be locked and there will be no escape. You'll be trained to fight by a *lanista* or 'butcher', an old gladiator whose fighting days are over.

GET FIT. You'll exercise every day with weights to build up your body's strength.

Before

After

Get stuck into it! It won't fight back you know!

FAKE SWORD. Until you can be trusted with a real weapon you will practice with a wooden sword.

HOW TO FIGHT. You'll learn how to fight with a sword, practising on a 'man of straw'. If you don't train hard enough you'll feel the sting of a whip on your back.

Man of straw

Rr..i..p

Handy hint

If you get injured, you must visit the school's excellent doctor. He'll dress your wounds and then you'll be ready to carry on training.

Who's who:

THE STAFF

Trainer *Owner* *Guard*

Mortician *Accountant* *Armourer* *Cook* *Doctor*

THE PUPILS

Slave *Criminal* *Condemned man* *Bankrupt Roman*

Get to know your place at the school. The staff are the bossy Romans looking after you – the pupils are the dregs of society.

11

Locked in! Your new family

Do you have the stomach for it?

Porridge

Barley grains

Beans

TRAINING doesn't end when you hang up your sword at the end of the day. You'll go back to your barracks – a long, low, wooden building. This is where you'll eat and sleep...and be locked in at night. Your trainer will come too and watch over you as you eat specially-prepared gladiator food. The trainer thinks of the men in the barracks as his family, so he will make sure you are looked after.

PORRIDGE. Every day the school cook will feed you on barley, porridge and boiled beans. Don't complain about boring, stodgy food – you'll get nothing else.

This stuff is only fit for dogs.

ASH. A few mouthfuls of dry, dusty ash are said to be good for building up the body. Just close your eyes and swallow. Don't choke!

YOUR TRAINER. He takes great pride in seeing how weak-bodied slaves can be turned into muscle-bound fighting men – but only if they follow a strict, nourishing diet. It's not for nothing that gladiators are sometimes called *hordearii*, which means 'barley men'.

Eat your porridge - you've got ash for pudding!

This isn't even fit for dogs!

Handy hint

Troubled by aches and pains? Then visit the school *unctore* who will massage your body.

MUSCLE MAN. Believe it or not, the school food really is good for you. All that porridge will give you muscles and strength.

13

Behave...or be punished

Punishments:

BRANDING. A runaway will have FHE (for *Fugitivus Hic Est*) and the initials of his owner, such as LT (for *Lucius Titius*), burned into his forehead. It means: 'This man is the runaway slave of Lucius Titius'.

FLOGGING. One hundred lashes of the whip will tear the skin from a runaway's back.

STOCKS. For a first offence you might be locked in the stocks for a week – time for you to learn to behave.

I T'S NO USE trying to escape, since the gladiators' school is surrounded by high walls and fences. You won't be able to climb over them without being spotted by the security guards. But, if you attack a member of staff, you will be punished. The school has a prison – a dark, rat-infested hole where prisoners are

> I never thought I'd miss that porridge.

shackled and chained to the walls. If you're unlucky enough to be locked inside, eat whatever the guards give you — it might be days before you get your next rotten meal. If you cause trouble too often your owner might sell you and you could end your days working in the mines. The choice is yours!

The prison has a low ceiling. There's not enough room to stand, so you have to lie or crouch on the ground.

On parade! The big day arrives

The night before:

BANQUET. You will be given a splendid feast – as much good food as you can eat. There will be meat and wine – definitely no porridge.

WHEN YOUR TRAINING is over, it is time for you to face the toughest challenge of your life. Your owner will take you, together with his other gladiators, to perform in the games. You will arrive in town the day before the games begin to have time to recover from the journey. That night you will be treated to a splendid meal. Enjoy it – it might be your last. On the day of the games you will march into the arena and parade before the emperor. Remember you are a gladiator – a courageous fighting man. Do not show any fear. There is silence as you call out the traditional words spoken by gladiators before the contest begins (right).

PUBLIC. The public view the gladiators at their banquet. They look for men who they think will fight well in the games and those who will not.

SAY GOODBYE. At the banquet some gladiators plead with the public to take final messages to their families.

ADVERTISEMENTS. Notices painted on walls announce the games. Street criers call out the names of the gladiators.

BANNERS. Men carry painted banners with details about the games to let everyone know they are about to begin.

17

Who's who in the arena?

What you will need:

Weapons

Spear

Dagger

Net

Lasso

Trident

Sword

Armour

Helmet

Greaves

Chain mail

Shields

Gladiators

ANDABATUS.
Wears a helmet
with no eye holes.
Charges blindly on
horseback at an
opponent.

ESSEDARIUS.
A gladiator who
drives a horse-
drawn chariot.

RETARIUS.
Tries to snare an
opponent in his net.
Left arm and
shoulder are
protected by armour.

MYRMILLO.
Carries a dagger
and shield.
Wears a wide
leather belt and
leg bands.

THRACIAN.
Uses a small
shield and a
curved dagger.
Wears greaves
on both legs.

IN YOUR TRAINING you will
have learned how to fight as one
particular type of gladiator. Perhaps
you were trained to fight as a
lightly-armoured *retarius* or 'net
man'. Or maybe your skills as an
essedarius – a chariot fighter – will be called
upon. It has cost your owner a lot of money
to buy you, feed, train and equip you for the
contest. Now you must be victorious – winning is all that matters.
If you lose, you die. So, be brave! Fight, conquer…and live!

Handy
hint

Make sure you have an attendant
to see to your needs. Let him carry
your equipment into the arena.

SAMNITE.
Wears a visored
helmet with
crest. Carries a
sword and a
large shield.

DIMACHAERIUS.
Fights with two
swords and wears
little armour.

LAQUERIUS.
Similar to a
retarius but
with a lasso
instead of a net.

SECUTOR.
A lightly armed
fighter who
chases his
opponent.

VELITUS.
Armed with
only a
spear.

WOMAN.
An uncommon
sight, but
women fight as
gladiators too.

Fight! Gladiators in action

Secutor *gladiator*

THE GAMES are about to begin. Your moment of glory is upon you – you hope. But first, you must entertain the crowd by fighting with blunt, wooden swords. Music sounds and your practice sword will be taken from you, to be replaced with a real weapon. You are about to fight for your life, but it is not just your opponent you have to worry about. Your trainer will be watching every move and, if he thinks you are not trying hard enough, he has a painful way of prodding you back into action.

This will teach you to run from a fight!

Prepare to fight

As you prepare for your fight, the arena will be buzzing with excitement. Don't let your nerves get the better of you – the show must go on!

WARM-UP FIGHT. First you'll fight with wooden swords in a practice duel.

GAMBLING. Spectators will gamble on whether you will win your fight …or not.

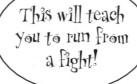

OPPONENT. You will be drawn to fight against another gladiator.

Retarius *gladiator*

Handy hint

Keep on fighting – if you don't your trainer will send a slave to whip you or prod you with a hot poker.

Fight, you lazy dog!

REAL WEAPON. You will be given your real weapon – no more wooden swords from now on.

MUSIC. Musicians will play war-trumpets, pipes, and flutes.

ACTION! The contest begins – it's a fight to the death.

NOISY CROWD. The crowd will cheer and shout all the time you are fighting.

Ouch! Let him have it!

BAD LUCK! In your contest you were drawn to fight a *retarius*, a gladiator who catches opponents in his net before moving in for the kill. As you lie on the sandy floor of the arena, he brings his dagger to your throat. You must think fast – you may have only seconds to live. The crowd are on their feet, shouting *"Habet, hoc habet!"*, which means "Got him! Let him have it!". There's only one thing you can do: appeal to the emperor. As you raise your left hand the emperor will turn to the crowd and let them decide your fate. All you can hope for is that they call out *"Mitte!"* – "Let him go!".

Will you live or die?

EMPEROR APPEAL. A fallen gladiator can appeal to the emperor by raising one finger on his left hand. The emperor will ask the crowd what they want.

THUMBS UP. If the crowd hold their thumbs up and wave their handkerchiefs, the fallen gladiator will be allowed to live.

THUMBS DOWN. If the crowd turn their thumbs to the ground, as if swiping a sword through the air, then the defeated man must die.

A DRAW. If both gladiators are still on their feet and have fought their best, then a draw may be declared and neither man will die.

Handy hint

Try and stay alive until midday. Then you'll have a chance for a rest when you'll be able to watch pairs of criminals fight to the death.

Splash!

Who are you?

Greek

Persian

ENEMIES. The Greek and Persian peoples were sworn enemies.

A sea battle

IT'S AN AMAZING SIGHT to see the arena flooded to make a lake. Water is piped in from a pool outside, then battleships called triremes float gracefully across it. A sea battle is about to begin,

Fighting at sea:

LONG AND SHORT RANGE. From a distance you will shoot burning arrows at the enemy ship. Then, when you are upon them, you will use hand weapons.

BATTERING RAM. The prow of a trireme is fitted with a bronze battering ram to smash into and sink other ships.

based on one fought between the Greeks and the Persians about 300 years ago. To entertain the crowd you will dress as either a Greek or Persian soldier. A sea battle is a great spectacle, so play your part well.

Handy hint

Learn to swim. Even though the water is shallow, you could still drown.

Prepare to perish, Persians!

Growl! Attacked by beasts

You will need:

BESTIARIUS. A gladiator trained to hunt wild beasts.

A FTER THE SEA BATTLE, the water is drained from the arena and another scene is set. The arena will become a park, with trees, rocky outcrops and wild beasts brought from Africa and other Roman provinces. An animal hunt will take place, where hunters stalk their prey with dogs and weapons. You must take great care – the animals are savage, hungry beasts.

Some *bestiarii* use weapons, but those who are criminals have no means of defence.

Aaargh!

WEAPONS. You hunt with spears, arrows, daggers, nets and fierce hunting-dogs.

Beware of the animals:

The arena will contain lions and tigers which can be taught to lick their tamer's hands and elephants that kneel before the emperor.

Handy hint

Know your escape routes! Look for a pole to climb up, a wall to jump over, or a cage to shelter inside.

Grrrr

Wait for it, wait for it...

Grrr...Grrrr

Let me at him! Let me at him!

It's over! The games end

T SEEMS THE CROWD showed you no mercy and the *retarius* was the winner of the contest. While your body is dragged from the arena, the victorious gladiator is presented with his prizes. At the end of the games, officials write up the record books, putting letters against the names of the competitors: 'P' means the person perished, 'V' stands for victor and 'M' indicates that the gladiator has lived to fight another day.

At the end of the day

CLEANERS. Boys rake the sand over to remove all signs of blood.

Victor today – back to porridge tomorrow!

If you are still alive...

PRIZES. Palm branches, silver dishes and gold are given to the gladiators who survive the games.

BACK FOR MORE. The owner of a winning gladiator will enter him in further contests.

DRAGGED AWAY. Men drag away the bodies of the dead and dump them in a pit.

FINISHED OFF. Dying gladiators are killed by a man dressed as the mythical character Charon.

Handy hint

After many victories a gladiator might be presented with a wooden sword. His fighting days will end and he can become a trainer at a gladiator school.

Glossary

Arena The building where gladiatorial games were held. It literally means 'sand' – a reference to the sand-covered floor.

Barbarian Anyone who was not a Roman. An uncivilised person.

Barracks The building in which gladiators lived while at training school.

Bestiarius A beast-fighter trained to hunt wild animals in the arena.

Chain mail A type of armour made from small, interlocking rings of metal.

Charon The ferryman who the Romans believed took the souls of the dead from the land of the living to the Underworld.

Galley A type of ship rowed by slaves.

Gallia An area of northern Europe where the present-day countries of France and Belgium are.

Games A form of public entertainment involving gladiators.

Gaul A member of one of the tribes that lived in Gallia.

Gladiator A man (or, very occasionally, a woman) trained to fight for the entertainment of others.

Greave A leg protector, usually made of metal, worn over the lower leg.

Hordearii A popular name for gladiators meaning 'barley men', due to the barley porridge they were fed on.

Lanista A man who trained or taught others to become gladiators.

Lasso A length of rope with a loop, used to catch an opponent.

Ludus gladiatorius A school or camp where gladiators lived and were trained how to fight.

Man of straw A post, sack, or framework which a gladiator practiced using his weapons against.

Mortician An undertaker. A person whose job it was to organise funerals.

Prow The front of a ship.

Sestertii Coins used in Roman currency.

Slave collar A name tag worn by slaves which stated who they belonged to.

Slingshot A hand-held weapon that hurled a small stone over a long distance.

Torque A loop of metal, often bronze or gold, worn around the neck as an item of jewellery.

Trident A three-pronged fishing spear.

Trireme A battleship of the Roman, Greek and Persian navies.

Unctore A person whose job it was to massage, or rub, soothing oils into someone's body.

Underworld The world of the dead according to Roman belief.

Index